Black Girl joy

Embrace the Journey

Affirmation Journal & Coloring Book

Nicole Lane

NEW YORK

The Birthing Place

JHP

This affirmation journal, and coloring book was created because of my love to color and my love for writing. Here in Black Girl Joy affirmations are what we use to speak life into our lives. They are meant for you to focus on and to begin creating a new mental mindset. I pray that you will use this as a guide to begin embracing the journey and the Joy of your life.

Black Girl *joy*

grateful AND *blessed*

Black Girl
joy

Philippians 4:8

Whatever things are true, noble, just, pure, lovely, of good report, any virtue, anything praiseworthy... Meditate on these things.

Affirmation
I invited gratitude into my life

_____

_____

_____

_____

_____

_____

_____

_____

_____

Affirmation
I deserve to be appreciated

_____

_____

_____

_____

_____

_____

_____

_____

_____

Affirmation
I am proud of who I am

_____

_____

_____

_____

_____

_____

_____

_____

_____

Affirmation
I am wealthy

_____

_____

_____

_____

_____

_____

_____

_____

_____

Affirmation
I am grateful for the gifts in my life

_____

_____

_____

_____

_____

_____

_____

_____

_____

Black Girl
joy

Black Girl *joy*

Affirmation
I am a gift

_____

_____

_____

_____

_____

_____

_____

_____

_____

Affirmation
I am blessed

_____

_____

_____

_____

_____

_____

_____

_____

_____

Affirmation
I am confident

_____

_____

_____

_____

_____

_____

_____

_____

_____

Affirmation
I choose to see the positive in me even in tough times

_____

_____

_____

_____

_____

_____

_____

_____

_____

Affirmation
I deserve peace

_____

_____

_____

_____

_____

_____

_____

_____

_____

Black Girl
joy

Black Girl *joy*

19

Affirmation
I willingly release all tension in my body

_____

_____

_____

_____

_____

_____

_____

_____

_____

Affirmation
It is safe for me to express my feelings

_____

_____

_____

_____

_____

_____

_____

_____

_____

Affirmation
I am content with every aspect of my life

_____

_____

_____

_____

_____

_____

_____

_____

Affirmation
I release the need to criticize my body

_____

_____

_____

_____

_____

_____

_____

_____

_____

Affirmation
I allow Peace and Joy to exist in all areas of my life

_____

_____

_____

_____

_____

_____

_____

_____

_____

Black Girl *joy*

> The **joy** of the **LORD** is my *strength*.
>
> Nehemiah 8:10

Black Girl
joy

26

Affirmation
Happiness is my birthright

_____

_____

_____

_____

_____

_____

_____

_____

_____

Affirmation
I deserve to live a joyful passionate life

_____

_____

_____

_____

_____

_____

_____

_____

Affirmation

Weeping may endure for a night, but Joy comes in the morning!

_____

_____

_____

_____

_____

_____

_____

_____

_____

_____

Affirmation
Today is a gift, and I embrace it with Joy

_____

_____

_____

_____

_____

_____

_____

_____

_____

Affirmation
I bring Joy with me wherever I go

_____

_____

_____

_____

_____

_____

_____

_____

_____

Black Girl *joy*

BY FAITH believe IN LOVE

Black Girl
joy

Affirmation
I choose to believe in my worth

Affirmation
I believe I will succeed

_____

_____

_____

_____

_____

_____

_____

_____

_____

Affirmation
I deserve to live a Joyful passionate life

_____

_____

_____

_____

_____

_____

_____

_____

_____

_____

Affirmation
I am abundant

_____

_____

_____

_____

_____

_____

_____

_____

_____

Affirmation
Under His Wings You Will Find Refuge

_____

_____

_____

_____

_____

_____

_____

_____

Black Girl
joy

Act Justly, Love Mercy, walk Humbly

Micah 6:8

Black Girl
joy

Affirmation
I am letting go of worries

_____

_____

_____

_____

_____

_____

_____

_____

_____

Affirmation
I am letting go of yesterday's sorrows

_____

_____

_____

_____

_____

_____

_____

_____

_____

Affirmation
I am learning to receive Gods love

_____

_____

_____

_____

_____

_____

_____

_____

_____

Affirmation
I am strong and overcome any obstacle that comes my way

_____

_____

_____

_____

_____

_____

_____

_____

_____

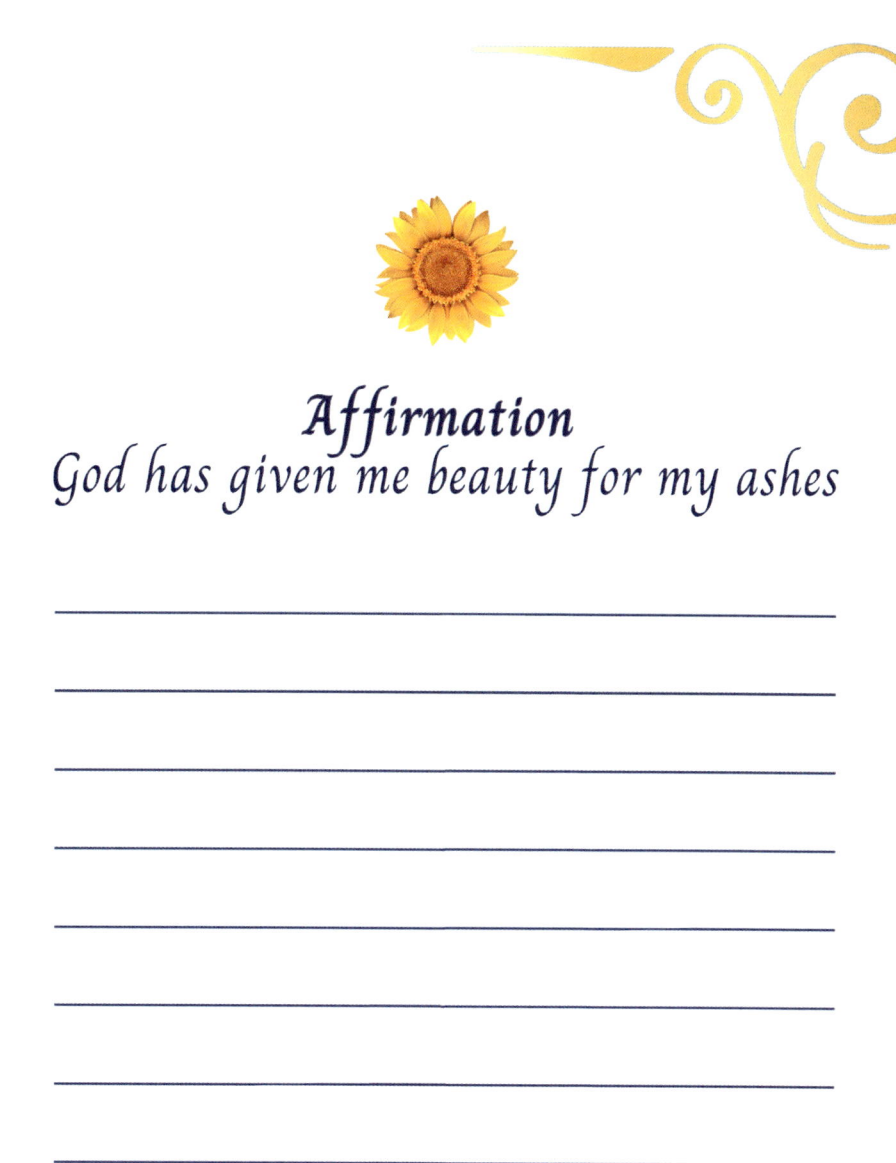

Affirmation
God has given me beauty for my ashes

_____

_____

_____

_____

_____

_____

_____

_____

_____

Black Girl *joy*

Our God is an Awesome God

Black Girl
joy

Affirmation
The Joy of the Lord is my strength

_____

_____

_____

_____

_____

_____

_____

_____

_____

Affirmation
Today is a gift and I embrace it with reassurance

_____

_____

_____

_____

_____

_____

_____

_____

_____

Affirmation
Joy is my birthright

_____

_____

_____

_____

_____

_____

_____

_____

_____

Affirmation
I am radiant, beautiful and thriving

_____

_____

_____

_____

_____

_____

_____

_____

_____

Affirmation
I will allow myself to dream big, knowing I am worthy

_____

_____

_____

_____

_____

_____

_____

_____

_____

Black Girl *joy*

53

Black Girl
joy

God cares
about the
BIG THINGS,
the small things,
and ALL things
in your life.

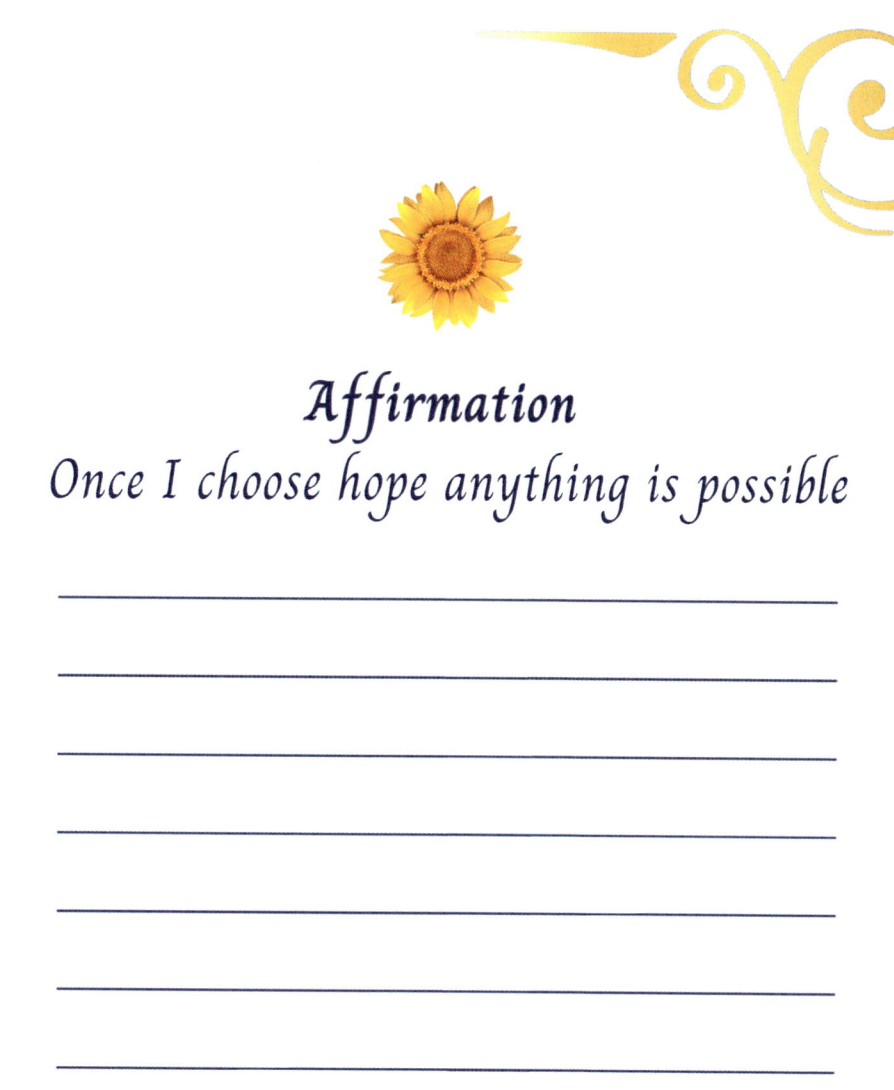

Affirmation
Once I choose hope anything is possible

_____

_____

_____

_____

_____

_____

_____

_____

_____

Affirmation
I forgive myself

_____

_____

_____

_____

_____

_____

_____

_____

_____

Affirmation
I know how to be still so I can hear from God

_____

_____

_____

_____

_____

_____

_____

_____

_____

_____

Affirmation
I am accepted by God

_____

_____

_____

_____

_____

_____

_____

_____

_____

Affirmation

I am not too much for God to handle. I am confident in Gods Power

_____
_____
_____
_____
_____
_____
_____
_____
_____
_____

Black Girl joy LLC

Connect With Us

Scan QR Code To Order

follow us on

Facebook · YouTube SUBSCRIBE · Instagram

All rights reserved. This book or any portion thereof may not be reproduced or used in any manner whatsoever without the express written permission of the publisher except for the use of brief quotations in a book review

Unless otherwise indicated, Scripture References are taken from the following:

New King James Version
Thomas Nelson

Artwork On Page 12, 40, 47:
designsbykemmy.com

Printed by Kindle Direct Publishing

First printing, 2024

Jana Hicks Publishing
New York

Made in the USA
Middletown, DE
04 May 2024